## WRITING AND STAGING

# Real-Life Plays

Charlotte Guillain

capstone

Edited by James Benefield
Designed by Philippa Jenkins
Original illustrations © Capstone Global Library Limited 2016
Picture research by Kelly Garvin
Production by Victoria Fitzgerald
Originated by Capstone Global Library Ltd
Printed and bound in China

19 18 17 16 15
10 9 8 7 6 5 4 3 2 1

**Library of Congress Cataloging-in-Publication Data**
Cataloging-in-publication data is available at the Library of Congress.
ISBN 978 1 4846 2771 6 (hardback)
ISBN 978 1 4846 2775 4 (paperback)
ISBN 978 1 4846 2779 2 (ebook PDF)

**Acknowledgments**
Photo credits: Alamy : Adrian Sherratt, 26, Chris Fredriksson, 35, redsnapper, 43; Capstone Press/Karon Dubke, cover, 25, 39, 41, 42; Corbis: Elder Ordonez/INFphoto.com, 12, Eric Fougere/VIP Images, 5, Hill Street Studios/Blend Images, 27, Robbie Jack, 30, Robert Wallace, 16; Dreamstime/Michael Gray, 29; Getty Images: Bestie Van der Meer, 23, Brent N. Clarke, 8, Christian Marquardt, 34, Emmanuel Faure, 22, Ernst Haas, 28, Hill Street Studios/Blend Images, 20, 24, 31, Keith Bernstein/The Weinstein Company, 14, Mario Ruiz/Time LIFE Images Collection, 4, Rod Morata, 17, ullstein bild, 33; Newscom: Christopher Aluka Berry/Rueters, 9; Shutterstock: archideaphoto, 36, dotshock, 7, godrick, 32, MANDY GODBEHEAR, 40, racorn, 10, S.V.Art, 19, sarra22, 37, Tracy Whiteside, 21; The Image Works: aka-images, 39 (bottom right), Nigel Norrington/ArenaPal, 18.

Artistic elements: Shutterstock: 3DDock.

We would like to thank Mike Gould for his invaluable contirbution to the book.

007486CTPSS16

# CONTENTS

Some words are shown in bold, **like this.** You can find out what they mean by looking in the glossary.

# WHAT IS A PLAY?

There are many ways we tell each other stories. People started out with **oral** stories, either passing on their version of real-life events or creating imaginary characters and worlds for younger generations. This way of sharing stories and information asked the audience to simply listen. Over time, the idea of **drama** developed, where groups of people began acting out a story onstage, in a play. Audiences of the play would both listen and watch.

## Remembering a story

To help people remember the stories, some storytellers began writing their tales down instead of just passing them on orally. Since these stories were recorded, it means we can know about them even though they may be hundreds or even thousands of years old! Some plays were also written down.

However, there is something very exciting about watching a story being acted out live and shared with lots of people. Many people also enjoy acting in plays, either as **professionals** or for fun.

These characters are in a real-life setting, in a play by Neil Simon.

This actor is playing the part of Mozart, the famous composer, in the play *Amadeus*.

Some playwrights like to write about their own real-life experiences. The American playwright Neil Simon wrote three partly **autobiographical** plays: *Brighton Beach Memoirs*, *Biloxi Blues*, and *Broadway Bound*. Each play is based on a different stage of his life, from growing up, to joining the army, to becoming a playwright.

Actors are not the only people involved in staging a play. They need a **director** to take the lead and make sure the actors work well as a team. Other people are needed to organize costumes, design **sets**, and manage the technical side of things, such as lighting and sound. Most plays start with a **playwright**, who chooses a story that he or she wants to tell and creates a play. Many playwrights write plays that are based on real people or events.

## What does the script of a play look like?

You don't have to be a professional playwright to write a play; you just need to understand how a **script** is put together to tell a story onstage. Playwrights write out their stories mostly in **dialogue** form. This format helps actors read and learn their **lines** more easily. The text is laid out so the names of the characters that are speaking appear on the left-hand side and their lines appear on the right. For example:

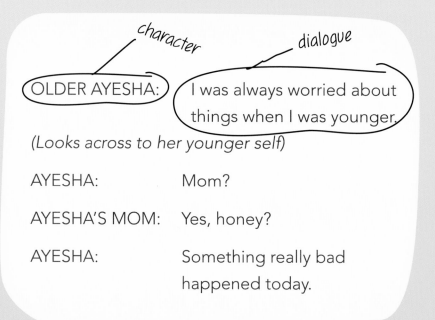

character

dialogue

OLDER AYESHA:      I was always worried about things when I was younger.

*(Looks across to her younger self)*

AYESHA:      Mom?

AYESHA'S MOM:      Yes, honey?

AYESHA:      Something really bad happened today.

You'll find other text in a play script, too. Playwrights also include **stage directions**, which tell the actors how to speak and move as they say their lines or react to other characters.

Try reading some play scripts to get used to how they are written.

Stage directions need to stand out from the dialogue, so they are usually in italics and appear inside parentheses *(like this)*. For example:

AYESHA'S MOM: *(putting down her phone)* Don't worry, you can tell me all about it.

*stage direction*

AYESHA: *(nervously)* Well, do you promise you won't be angry?

AYESHA'S MOM: *(frowning)* It depends what you're going to tell me!

## Writing Tip

Scripts for plays based on real people or events often include the use of real dialogue or quotations. A playwright may directly interview people involved in an event in the past or read **transcripts** of interviews made at the time of an event. If a playwright decides to make up dialogue, he or she would make sure the language used is historically accurate. To do this, the playwright would read **biographies** or watch videos from the period.

# PLAYS BASED ON REAL LIFE

If you want to write a play based on real life, you need to choose which story you want to tell before you start writing. You could base your play on real events that have happened to you or your friends. Perhaps you want to write a play about a famous person, either alive today or from history. Alternately, you may want to set your play during a real event—for example, during the Revolutionary War or at the time of the 2015 Nepalese earthquake. Make sure the story you choose really inspires you and is something you think people would want to see.

## Why write about real life?

There are many reasons why playwrights write about real life:

- Writing a play about real events can be a good way to look at different points of view of what happened.

- It gets the audience thinking about an important issue.

- It asks the audience to consider how to behave in certain situations.

- Some plays based on real life can also be a way to celebrate and remember an important person's life or a historic event.

This historical play, *Wolf Hall*, is based on the life of England's King Henry VIII and his advisors.

Many plays and movies are based on important people's lives. David Oyelowo played the part of Martin Luther King, Jr.

For hundreds of years, playwrights have dealt with big **themes** that have made audiences think. William Shakespeare wrote many plays, some based on real people such as England's King Henry V, and others created from made-up stories. All his plays include important themes that still affect people today, such as love, jealousy, and death. Before you write your script, you may want to think about what themes you'd like to cover in your story.

*The Miracle Worker* is a play by the American playwright William Gibson. The story is based on the life of Helen Keller, who became blind and deaf as an infant, and the way a woman named Anne Sullivan helped her learn to communicate.

## Ideas for a play based on real life

There are many places you can get ideas for your play. You could:

- base your script on events you have studied in history class at school or watched on television

- bring to life an event that happened to an older family member when he or she was young

- take a situation that has happened to you in school or an event that you have read about in the newspaper.

The important thing is to do as much research as possible about the event or situation on which you are basing your play, so you can retell it in a believable way.

You might have a relative with a life story that is a great starting point for a play.

Many young people encounter bullying at some point in school. So perhaps you could write a play about this issue and help your audience to talk about it. You could make people think about how they would react if they saw other people being bullied. It's a good idea to start by making an outline to show what will happen in your play.

## Writing Tip

Remember, even if you choose to base your play on a real-life event, you don't need to show every detail of what happened during it. You can just focus on a particular part of the story to make your play more exciting. You could also leave out certain parts to give your play **pace** and keep audiences on the edge of their seats.

Ayesha starts at a new school. She knows one person there—Madison. But Madison's friend, Katy, isn't happy.

Katy tells the other students lies about Ayesha.

Katy steals Ayesha's notepad and sends nasty notes to Madison.

Madison and Ayesha argue. Ayesha is sad. Another girl, Sarah, comforts Ayesha and tells her she saw Katy take the notepad.

Ayesha confronts Katy. Katy explains she is jealous of Ayesha. Ayesha tells Katy all three of them can be friends. Ayesha includes Sarah in their group.

Ayesha notices Katy sneaking Madison's earrings into Ayesha's bag.

The actor Bradley Cooper is performing in a play called *The Elephant Man,* based on a real person's experience.

## Creating characters based on real people

If you're writing a play based on a real-life event or real people, you have to put in extra effort when creating your characters. Spend some time researching what people are, or were, like in the time period you want to write about. Below are some suggestions to help you create realistic and believable characters:

- Read books about the people who will appear in your play.

- Meet them in person if you can.

- Get a sense of how these people talk, their **mannerisms**, as well as what they look like and the sort of clothes they wear.

- If your story is set in the past, make sure your characters fit that time. They need to speak in an appropriate away and not use modern **slang**. It can be hard to write dialogue to match how people spoke hundreds of years ago. A good place to start is by watching other plays or movies from that time period to get some ideas.

List the key characters in your play. Make some notes about their personalities and what matters to them. For example:

**Ayesha**
* The main character
* The audience should like her and relate to how she's feeling
* Strong and thoughtful, she confronts the bully at the end

**Madison**
* Ayesha's friend
* A lot of fun and likes to make everyone laugh
* Quite loud, but underneath she's not very confident

**Sarah**
* Quiet and shy, she doesn't talk to other students unless she has to
* Observant
* She has a strong sense of right and wrong and will speak up about it

**Katy**
* Madison's friend
* Worries she'll lose her friendship with Madison when Ayesha joins their school
* Bullies Ayesha, but becomes aware of her actions
* Apologizes when Ayesha confronts her at the end

# WRITING A PLAY BASED ON REAL LIFE

The **plot** of a play is what happens in the story. When playwrights write about a famous person, they may choose to include a number of important moments in that person's life or focus on just one key event. For example, if you are writing a play about Nelson Mandela, you may want to show him being arrested, his life in prison, and his time as president of South Africa.

Be clear about the order in which events happen so that you don't get them mixed up. It might help to make a timeline to show the order of events as you are writing the play.

This is a scene from a movie about Nelson Mandela, *Mandela: Long Walk to Freedom.*

## Keep it simple

It is much easier to write your script and stage your play if you keep things simple. A straightforward, **linear** plot is easy for the audience to follow. Most of the time, your characters will speak among themselves. However, you can get them to address the audience directly. This will help make the plot clear to your audience and explain the characters' behaviors.

You could also have a separate **narrator** to speak to the audience. A narrator is removed from the characters in the story, so he or she can comment on what is happening onstage and link one event to another.

In *The Bully*, the characters speak to the audience and among themselves:

SARAH: *(to the audience)* I felt bad that nobody was talking to Ayesha. I had to tell her what I saw.

AYESHA: *(to herself)* I don't understand what's happened. I've never felt so alone…

SARAH: *(to Ayesha)* Hi, Ayesha—are you okay? Do you want to play? There's something I'd like to tell you…

## The shape of your script

It is good for your play to have a beginning, middle, and end. Introduce your characters at the start of the play, then build **tension** as the play moves along. The main character should encounter a problem near the middle. Some real-life events may not have a clear beginning, middle, and end. However, you can choose which parts of the story to include, to give your play clear sections.

As you move toward the story's end, your characters should try to deal with the problem. The story should finish with either a happy or sad ending. The end of the play is called the **resolution**, when the problem has been dealt with and people can move on. Of course, not all real-life stories have a happy ending, but you can still show your audience that your characters have learned something along the way.

The play *War Horse* is based on Michael Morpurgo's novel. It tells the story of a horse sent to the battlefront in World War I. It is fiction, but based on real events and experiences. The ending of the play is happy, but there's sadness along the way. The play reflects the reality that millions of people and many horses died in World War I.

You want to keep your audience interested, so keep your plot moving at a good pace.

Think about how you can build up to a moment of tension, or the main character's **low point**, when it seems like nothing will go right. Then figure out how to reach the resolution from there.

## The structure of *The Bully*

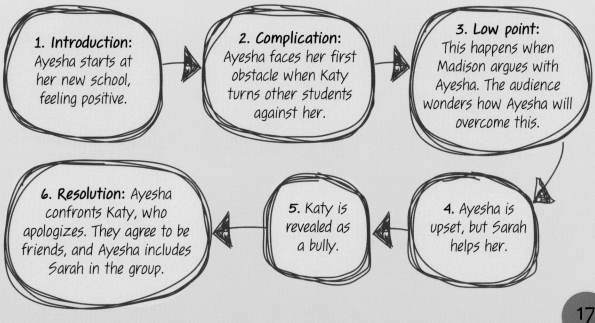

**1. Introduction:** Ayesha starts at her new school, feeling positive.

**2. Complication:** Ayesha faces her first obstacle when Katy turns other students against her.

**3. Low point:** This happens when Madison argues with Ayesha. The audience wonders how Ayesha will overcome this.

**6. Resolution:** Ayesha confronts Katy, who apologizes. They agree to be friends, and Ayesha includes Sarah in the group.

**5.** Katy is revealed as a bully.

**4.** Ayesha is upset, but Sarah helps her.

## Speaking parts

The dialogue in a play based on real events should sound natural. If your play is about people your age in today's society, you could record yourself talking with friends and then try to base your characters' dialogue on the words you would use with your own friends. Your script will sound more realistic if your characters talk the way people speak normally.

Characters will speak differently than the way we talk today in a play set years ago, as this one is.

You can record your friends talking to help make your play's dialogue sound natural. Try using a dictaphone or a cell phone to do this.

## Writing Tip

If your play is in a modern, familiar setting, tell your actors about the characters and their situations and let them **improvise**, using the script as inspiration. Actors should behave like the characters in the script. However, they could make up their own words rather than following the script precisely. Listening to what they say when they improvise might help you to write more natural dialogue.

While the dialogue in historical plays needs to sound realistic, some plays based on historical events might have words that are hard to say. Some playwrights might tell performers how to say these words in several notes before the play begins. These notes are not meant to be read out loud during the play.

## Using slang in dialogue

A play set in a school in the present day would appear odd if the dialogue doesn't sound natural. If the characters' lines are even slightly out of date, the audience will pick up on this. If the dialogue is unrealistic, the audience won't believe in the situation.

Young people use more slang than adults, and the dialogue in a play like *The Bully* should reflect this. Don't go over the top, but try to use a few **colloquial** expressions that everyone in the audience will be able to understand. This will make it feel like a version of real life.

# DIRECTING A PLAY

Once the play is written, the next step is to find a director. The director leads a team of actors and **crew** to bring the play to life. He or she gets the play ready for a performance in front of an audience.

The director chooses which actors will play each character. He or she also finds people to keep things running backstage—for example, a set designer, a costume designer, and technical engineers in lighting and sound. The director leads the rehearsals, decides when each part of the play will be practiced, and asks the actors to speak and move in certain ways.

## TRY IT

If you are directing a play based on an event that is familiar to everyone, you may want to work with your actors to share ideas about how each character should behave and look. It may be a good idea to organize **workshops** before you start rehearsing. Here, you can find how each actor could **portray** and dress as his or her character.

The director discusses with actors how they should be positioned onstage.

Everyone on the team should know the script well.

## Ways to direct

Below are some things a director should consider when directing a play like *The Bully*:

- Read the script with everyone on the team. Talk about each character and discuss the play's story. Has anyone on the team experienced a similar problem? Talk about what people did and how they felt. Encourage people to ask questions and think about what they would do in that situation.

- Consider how you can show the school setting in this play. It's probably a good idea to have a simple set, using basic furniture and **props,** to show where the characters are and what is happening. In terms of costumes, your actors could be wearing what they normally wear to school. Find people to take charge of set design, costumes, props, lighting, and sound.

- Hold **auditions** to see who would like to act in the play, and decide which actor will play which **part.**

## Auditions

As the director, you need to hold auditions to **cast** the play. Actors turning up to the auditions will probably want to try out for particular **roles**.

Talk to the actors about the real-life situation in the play. Ask them if they can speak in an appropriate accent, or if they can understand why certain characters feel the way they do. If your play is based on a specific historical period, be aware that life would have been quite different back then, compared to today. For example, women may not have had much independence or freedom. It is important that your actors understand this and can **empathize** with the characters they play.

## THEATER JOB

Professional theater and movie companies use a **casting director** to find actors. A casting director is helpful, especially when many actors are needed for a play. He or she makes a list of possible actors for the important parts and shows this to the director, before organizing auditions.

Try to make the actors feel relaxed when they audition.

You might not get the part you wanted, but another part might be a better fit.

If more than one actor tries out for a part, you need to decide who is the best fit for each role. Maybe a very confident actor would be better for a loud character than a quieter, more thoughtful actor. If your play features famous historical people, think about which actors look most like the characters! Try to find parts for everyone who wants to act, even if they only have a nonspeaking part.

## Casting *The Bully*

Here are some suggestions for things to consider when casting a play like *The Bully*:

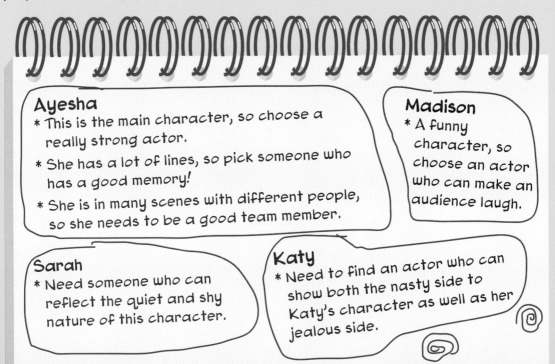

**Ayesha**
* This is the main character, so choose a really strong actor.
* She has a lot of lines, so pick someone who has a good memory!
* She is in many scenes with different people, so she needs to be a good team member.

**Madison**
* A funny character, so choose an actor who can make an audience laugh.

**Sarah**
* Need someone who can reflect the quiet and shy nature of this character.

**Katy**
* Need to find an actor who can show both the nasty side to Katy's character as well as her jealous side.

# ACTING IN A PLAY BASED ON REAL LIFE

When you start rehearsing a play based on real events, it can be useful to try some improvisation. This means letting your actors get into their characters and talk to each other without a script. They could pretend to be in a certain situation from the play and explore what they think and feel. This helps the actors to get a feel for their characters and to understand why they, and the other characters, behave the way they do.

## TRY IT

Improvisation is a good time for your actors to show off any historical research they have done! For example, if an actor knows that his or her character was an angry person who made decisions from an emotional response, he or she can share this information with others.

You can have fun improvising!

## Improvisation games

Try these games to help explore your play and its characters:

### "The Object Game"

1. Get your actors to each find an object from a selection and explain to the rest of the group how it links to his or her character. For example, an actor could hold up an old broken box. This could represent the way the character keeps making mistakes and hiding his or her feelings away.

2. Each actor should talk about his or her character in the third person—for example, "He thinks this..." or "She feels like this..."

### "Talking to the Wall"

1. Each actor should imagine that his or her character is alone in a room. The actor must tell the story of the play from the character's perspective. He or she could face the wall and speak to it as if it were a good listener or friend.

2. Ask the actor how he or she feels afterward: Bitter? Angry? Thankful? Or something else?

3. Encourage the group to provide feedback after each person has "talked to the wall." Have they learned anything new about the characters?

25

## Practice makes perfect!

When you are staging a play, you need to rehearse it before you can perform in front of an audience. As the director, you should make a rehearsal schedule as early as possible, so your whole team knows what dates and times they are needed.

You have to work hard in rehearsals, but they can be fun, too.

## TRY IT

When an actor has a lot of lines to learn in a play, it can feel overwhelming. But tell your actors not to worry too much—they might be surprised by what they can remember! Encourage them to start by reading their lines out loud. They should ask someone to test them on their lines and read the **cues**. Another useful tip is to record their lines so that they can listen back whenever they get a chance.

Actors feel much more confident when they have learned their lines.

In rehearsals, the director often starts by getting the actors to practice certain scenes in the play before running through the whole play. To begin with, actors can read from the script, but they will need to learn their lines as soon as possible.

For actors who are not needed to rehearse a particular scene, it's still important to show respect for the others who are. Encourage actors to stay behind sometimes and watch others rehearse, so that everyone understands the whole story of the play. People can often pick up some good tips by watching others.

If your play is set in a particular historical period, it's a good idea to encourage your actors to read about that period while they're waiting for their turn in rehearsal. This will help to keep everyone in the world of the play. You could hang up pictures of famous historical people from that period backstage. This will help everyone to remember what their characters should be like throughout the rehearsals.

# BEHIND THE SCENES

Most plays have a set that shows the audience where the scenes are taking place. It is the job of the set designer to create the set, with guidance from the director. Together, you need to think about the setting for your play and how you can share this with the audience.

The play *Red* by John Logan is about the artist Mark Rothko. Rothko created striking paintings that used color in a bold way. Throughout the performance, there is a huge blank canvas onstage that the actors gradually paint in red. This shows how Rothko worked, but it also creates a changing set that is quite simple.

Professional theaters can have fancy sets and costumes.

A young theater group made this simple set.

## Designing scenery

Make some sketches and talk to others involved in the play for scenery ideas. Think about how you can create the idea of a place in a simple way. For example, you could give an idea of a town by painting the silhouette of rooftops on a **backdrop**.

If your play is based on a real event similar to your everyday life, then you may be able to borrow items to show where the play is set. In a play based in a school, like *The Bully*, you will probably want to make your stage look like a classroom. You can do this by putting up posters taken from a real classroom in your school or asking permission to borrow tables and chairs from a classroom.

Even if your play is based on a real person or event from history, it's still possible to create a good look. For example, you could just use one or two colors in the background, plus lighting and props, such as a candlestick or a quill pen, to give a sense of time and mood.

## Costumes

Unless your play is set in another time in history or in another part of the world, it should be fairly easy to organize costumes, since they will probably just be ordinary clothes. As director, you need to choose someone to be the costume manager. He or she can check with the actors to find what clothes they already have that may be suitable for their characters. Borrow clothes from each other and try to get any extra pieces from garage sales or thrift stores.

Many plays about real-life events need historical costumes.

The costume manager needs to keep everyone's costume ready to wear.

If your play is set in the past or in a different country, it might be harder to get realistic costumes. One way to get around this is to dress all the actors in black and just use makeup, hats, and props to show that the action is taking place in a different time or place. If you want to have real costumes, you could look into renting or borrowing costumes from a local theater group. Your school may also have costumes from previous productions that you could use.

## Costumes for *The Bully*

A play like *The Bully* shouldn't cause too many problems with costumes. The characters can wear their own clothes. If they wear school uniforms, they all need to look the same, since the characters go to the same school. Ayesha's mom and her teacher should wear the type of clothes an adult wears to work. You don't need to use much makeup, apart from what you need to stop the actors' faces from looking too pale under stage lights.

Make sure nobody touches the props table without permission.

## Props

Props are objects that the actors use as they act. Normally one person, called the props manager, is in charge of organizing props.

The props manager needs to be organized. He or she makes sure all the props needed in the play are found and keeps them in one place—such as on a table offstage—where they can be picked up easily by the actors. After rehearsals and performances, the props manager makes sure all the props are gathered up and put back in the right place so that nothing gets lost.

Go through the script and make a list of all the objects the actors use during the play. If your play is based on your own experience, it should be easy to gather props from friends and family. However, if your play is based on a historical event or set in another part of the world, it might be more difficult.

You could make your own props or use simple objects to represent certain items. You could even mime your actions instead of using props.

## Props for *The Bully*

It shouldn't be too hard to find the props for a play set in a school. Here are some ideas:

- School backpacks: Actors playing the parts of the students can bring their own backpacks.

- Notebooks: Choose a type of notebook that you think the character would use himself or herself; its design could even match the way the character is dressed.

- Earrings: These are going to be so small it's unlikely the audience will be able to see them, so your actors could just mime taking them on and off.

It might be easier to have little or no real food onstage, to keep things simple.

### TRY IT

Sometimes you may have to eat during a scene. This can be tricky: you don't want to miss a line just because you're still chewing! Take small mouthfuls so you can eat quickly. If you're worried about getting hiccups, you could always mime eating!

## Lighting in a play based on real life

As the director, you need to choose people to be in charge of the lighting for your play. Stage lighting can range from complicated systems and rows of lights in professional theaters to simple lights in a school auditorium. Even simple lights can be effective if they're used at the right moments in a play. For example, use a bright light to represent daytime and dim light for nighttime.

Lights can also create atmosphere: a darker stage fits a scary or sad moment in the play. Dim or flickering lights could be used to represent candlelight in a historical play.

You can position lights to create shadows. This suggests a certain type of day or adds to the atmosphere.

Some plays and musicals have musicians playing live. Sometimes they sit in an orchestra pit.

## Sounds in a play based on real life

It's important to think about the music you might use in a play based on real life. Choose someone to be your sound engineer, who will work with you on the music and sound effects. Music clips can be stored in files on a computer or on a CD.

In a historical play, it would be good to play music from the period where it is set. For example, if your play is about World War II, you could play songs from the 1940s. If you want to use popular music, be aware that a lot of music is under **copyright**. This means you have to pay the person who created it when you use it in a performance. To get around this, you could ask friends who play in a band or orchestra to play music during your performance, or create and record your own sounds and music.

## THEATER JOB

Lighting and sound technicians need to be very organized and good with technology. They also need to be good at concentrating, because they'll have to listen for cues to turn effects on and off. There can also be a lot of sitting still for a long time!

# COLLECTING SOUNDS

If you don't want to pay to use music in your play, you could collect and record your own sound effects and music instead.

1. Make sure you have some good recording equipment. You may be able to use your cell phone or tablet, or borrow a microphone and recording device from your school.

2. Next, make a list of all the sound effects in your play. If your play is set in a school, these sounds might include chair legs scraping on the floor, students talking, the bell ringing, teachers talking, and the sound of people moving around the school hallways.

3. Ask permission to make recordings of these sounds in your school. It's best if you record the sounds happening naturally and don't ask people to make them specially.

You might be surprised by how many different sounds there are around you in school.

If you have a friend who plays an instrument, ask him or her to record some music for your play.

4. Think about other sounds and music you could add to your play to create atmosphere. You could record a friend playing a few chords on a guitar and play this at the start of each new scene. In a play like *The Bully*, you may need the sound of cell-phone ringtones.

5. Make sure you save the sounds and give the files clear names, so that you can easily find and organize them on a computer for the big night.

## TRY IT

Some plays are performed on the radio. Radio listeners can hear but can't see what is happening. To make radio plays more convincing and help the audience figure out the location of a scene, people have to create realistic sound effects in a small studio. For example, they may put some gravel in a tray and stomp on it to show someone walking along a gravel path. They might even flap a pillow to make it sound like a flying bird!

# FINISHING TOUCHES

It's very important to **publicize** your play. This means telling as many people as possible about it, so that a big audience turns up to your performance. For example:

- If your play is based on local events, you should think about how it connects to people living locally who might be interested.

- Is your play about a situation that people are likely to have experienced themselves? For example, if your play is about bullying and you perform it during anti-bullying week, more people are likely to hear about it and go to see it.

- If your play is based on a historical event, you can create extra interest if you perform it around the same time as a special anniversary of that event.

Make sure you think about all the connections you can make before you start to publicize your play.

## TRY IT

Other ways to spread the word about your play include handing out **fliers**, putting an advertisement in a local newspaper, and writing an article for your school or community newsletter.

## THE BULLY

Directed by Michael Roberts

A tale of insecurity, jealousy, and acceptance!

**STARRING**

**DAISY WHITE** as Katy

**RACHAEL SIM** as Ayesha

**JANE ROBERTS** as Madison

Thursday, Friday, and Saturday, June 5—7, at 6 p.m.
at Yorktown Academy
e-mail the main office

*title of play*

*director*

*people playing the main characters*

*where and when the performance is*

*how you get tickets*

## Making posters

Make a poster to tell people about your play. The words on your poster need to make it very clear what the play is about. You want people to come and see it, so think about what you could include to encourage that. A photograph of the actors in rehearsals or a strong image that represents the message of your play can be very striking. If your play is based on a historical person or event, the style of the poster could be influenced by that period. For example, if your play is about the civil rights activist Rosa Parks, you could include a black and white photo on your poster or a **font** that was commonly used in the 1950s. Make sure you also include the location, date, and time of the performances!

Plays have been written about the civil rights activist Rosa Parks to remind people of what she achieved.

## Final preparation

At last, the date of your first performance is getting near! It's time to fix any little problems that keep coming up in rehearsals; don't ignore anything that keeps going wrong. Try to find solutions so that things run smoothly.

It might be a good idea to get some trusted adults to watch a rehearsal and give you some feedback, in case there is anything you haven't spotted that could be improved. You may want to practice certain scenes more often if they are especially tricky or if people keep making mistakes in them.

Make sure everyone knows what they want to do and feels happy about it.

Your dress rehearsal should be as close to a real performance as possible.

Sometimes your actors may need a little break. Rehearsing and learning lines can be very tiring, and everyone starts to feel nervous and stressed out as the first performance gets nearer. It might be a good idea to take some time out from the play and do something else for a day or two. This way, everyone can come back fresh and ready to perform.

Make sure you have a **dress rehearsal** so that everyone is comfortable with their costumes and confident using all the props. You'll also need to have a **technical rehearsal** to focus on lighting and sound.

## TRY IT

It's a good idea to invite a small audience along to your dress rehearsal, so that the actors can get used to performing in front of people. This "test" audience may react to the play in ways that the actors hadn't predicted, which can make a difference to the feel of the play. It will really help to prepare your actors before the first live performance takes place.

# GO FOR IT!

Congratulations—it's time to perform your play! By the time you reach this point, you will all have worked very hard, writing the script, learning the lines, rehearsing, and organizing everything behind the scenes. Staging a play is a huge team effort. It's a great achievement to get to the point where you can perform it for an audience.

If your play is about a real event or person, remind yourselves what the real story was as you get ready to perform. Read quotations, watch documentaries, and look at photos to really get under the skin of the person. If your play is based on a real experience that you and your audience members are likely to recognize, remind yourselves of the improvising you did at the start of rehearsals. Remember the feelings you talked about there and try to empathize with all the characters in the play. Finally, take some time to think about the world of your play before you step onto the stage for the first performance.

The audience is about to arrive. Are you excited?

42

It's a great feeling to work as part of a team when you perform your play.

You could even invite the people who inspired your play, or local historians who are interested in that time period, to watch the performance. When you are designing your **program** for the play, you might ask these people to write something about the real event or person behind your play, as an introduction!

Finally, remember to have fun. You won't forget writing and staging your first play or the friends you made along the way!

## TRY IT

If you made changes at the dress rehearsal, make sure you rehearse the new version of the play before opening night. An audience can react to a play in ways you weren't expecting. This test run will help you prepare for the first real performance.

# GLOSSARY

**audition**  test for actors to try out for particular roles

**autobiographical**  story about the writer's own life

**backdrop**  background to a set

**biography**  story about someone else's life

**cast**  give actors roles in a play; the collective name for all the actors in a play

**casting director**  person who decides which actor would be best for each role

**colloquial**  informal way of speaking

**copyright**  legal right to use a piece of music, writing, or art

**crew**  people working backstage on a play

**cue**  signal to an actor to move or speak

**dialogue**  words actors speak

**director**  person in charge of staging a play

**drama**  type of play, usually serious in subject matter

**dress rehearsal**  final rehearsal run, in costume, as if it is a performance

**empathize**  understand the feelings of others

**flier**  small leaflet giving information

**font**  set of letters and symbols in a particular design

**improvise**  make up a sketch as you go along

**line**  sentence of dialogue in the script

**linear**  following a clear sequence

**low point**  hero's worst moment in the play

**mannerism**  way of behaving

**narrator**  person who describes and explains what is happening

**oral**  spoken story told out loud from memory

**pace**  moving at a steady speed

**part**  role in a play

**playwright**  person who writes the text of the play

**plot**  story of a book, movie, or play

**portray**  show something

**professional**  person paid to do something

**program**  booklet for audience members giving information about the play, cast, and crew

**prop**  object that actors can move around onstage

**publicize**  spread information about an event

**resolution**  moment where obstacles are overcome

**role**  character or part in a play

**script**  text of the play

**set**  scenery and furniture on the stage

**slang**  informal language

**stage direction**  instruction for an actor in a play script

**technical rehearsal**  practice that focuses on sound, lighting, and use of props

**tension**  emotional strain and stress

**theme**  key idea

**transcript**  written copy of spoken words

**workshop**  drama produced through group discussion and improvisation

# FIND OUT MORE

## Web sites

FactHound offers a safe, fun way to find Internet sites related to this book. All of the sites on FactHound have been researched by our staff.

Here's all you do:

Visit www.facthound.com
Type in this code: 9781484627716

Most cities and many towns have theater companies that put on plays for kids. Do research to find the theaters near you that offer plays for kids or theater training for young people. Perhaps you could ask if you could visit and look around, or ask about plays that are coming up. Check to see if there are any workshops with the actors or the writers.

## Plays to read

Kane, Bob. *Acting Scenes & Monologues For Kids!* Burbank, CA: Burbank Publishing, 2010.

Parker, Douglas M. *Contemporary Monologues for Young Actors.* Seattle: CreateSpace, 2014.

Think about some historical figures or events that you find interesting. Also think about your own life and the sorts of issues that affect you and interest you. With an adult's help, you can do research to find plays that address these stories and issues. If you can't find the exact play you have in mind, you can always write your own!

## Drama games

If you enjoyed the "The Object Game" and the "Talking to the Wall" improvisation games earlier in the book, perhaps try the following improvisation game, too.

### "The Clapping Game"

1. Everyone should stand in a circle.

2. The teacher or director asks the person on his or her left to clap. The person on his or her left should also clap, and so on, until the clap reaches the teacher or director who first clapped.

3. Get the group to see how fast they can all do this and time it.

Try playing this game with another sound or an object.

# INDEX